Panorama-Books: PEKING

D1097749

With thirty colour plates

OTTO CONSTANTINI

PEKING

The Old Imperial City

Introduction by

TILEMANN GRIMM

Translated by G. A. Colville

Distributed by

DOUBLEDAY & COMPANY, INC.
GARDEN CITY, NEW YORK

Wrapper and cover designed by Gerhard M. Hotop

The photo "Imperial City in winter" is from Magnum

The wall it is that leaves behind the first lasting impression — the massive, 40 ft.-high wall that surronds the city of Peking. In the early days, one first approached it from the east, from the direction of T'ung-chou; to which the Imperial canal on which one travelled in the leisurely tempo of a more comfortable age extended. Later on, the railway came up to the city from the south. And now today the airliner circles over the airport in the northwest of the town, before starting to land. It is always the wall that, as a structure rising up suddenly out of the plain and crowned with gateway- and corner-towers, or as long-drawn-out double square, lies to air passengers so distinctly at their feet. In Chinese "wall" also means "town". It is one and the same thing. A town is the form of human settlement surrounded by a wall.

There is still another word the character of which exhibits a square, walled-round area. The word today means "country" (kuo), but it once signified a lord's seat, a citadel, dominating the surrounding countryside. That was the time when warlike tribes, penetrating from the north and northwest, dominated under a loose feudal system the race of peasant-farmers living in the North Chinese lowlands. This was the beginning of Chinese history as we know it. It extends back as a far as the second millenium B. C.

Peking's size and importance as a capital is due to warlike tribes thrusting in from the north: first the Kitan (about the year 1000 A. D.); after whom the Russian language still calls China and the Chinese (Kitai). These were followed by Tunguse Djurdjans, who ruled under the Chinese dynastic name of "Chin", the "Golden Ones", and, finally, the Mongolians. These made Peking a world capital for the first time. From here, Kublai Khan ruled almost all of Asia and the fringes of Europe. Travellers from the farthest West saw the city that was the most magnificent of their times. Marco Polo described it and was derided as an exaggerator "Messer Milione". And at the beginning of the fourteenth century Giovanni de Montecorvino was the first Catholic Archbishop of Peking.

Pe-king: that means "northern capital". It was not always so called. Indeed, it was once called Nan-king, capital of the south, as is the name today of the city on the lower reaches of the Yangtse when the Kitan, under their Chinese dynastic name of "Liao", coming here from the northern steppes, built up here their empire, in which the city was the southernmost. The succeeding Djurdjans, or Chin-Tartars, called the city the "central capital" because they had been able to extend their domination farther to the south. And the Mongols called it in Chinese "Ta-tu", the "great capital". A rectangle 4 miles by 4³/₄ miles, it fell when it was conquered during the national revolution of the later Ming dynasty, when their own capital was transferred to the south, to Nanking. And not until the third Emperor of the dynasty, whose reign was called "Eternal Joy" (Yung-lo), was the capital re-transferred to the north, built up, and called the northern capital. That was in the year 1421, since when it has so remained, except for a short period between 1928 and 1948. Nor have the outlines of the town much changed since. Thus, as today we make our acquaintance with Peking, its palaces, its temples, its parks and its most important highways, we may remember that it has been the capital of the last two dynasties to rule the already old Chinese empire for more than a full five hundred years.

And in the meantime Peking itself has become old. In the faces of its inhabitants is mirrored that resignation that can be bestowed on men who experience so many blows of fate. The new fades away as the old has already faded away, and who knows what can lie in store? When, after the 1911 revolution that did away with the thousand-year-old monarchical form of State, the mighty sign on the main gate of the city was taken down for another to be erected, no one quite knew what to do with the old one and it was dragged up inside the gateway tower to the floor of the roof. There, however, another one already lay. When they blew the dust off it a little they discovered it was the old sign dating from the Ming dynasty that had to step down in 1644. Perhaps this story is only made up, but it is a good story. Peking has grown very old.

Yet it was not too old to fade away before the irresistible encroachment of modern times. It was made the site of the first Chinese university even in the final years of the last dynasty. From its lecture-rooms came a young generation which set about breaking with its own past, becoming more and more radical every year. The "New Youth", the periodical which proclaimed for the first time the theses of a new epoch in the intellectual world of China, was born in Peking. The first number appeared in 1915, when Europe was clutched in the agony of a stalement in material conflict. The year 1919 marked the first public outbreak of this young generation. The intellectual revolution of China arose as a result of a political procession of protest. This procession took place in Peking. The Peking University was the centre of this movement. Sun Yatsen, the spiritual father of the New China, died in 1925 in Peking, as though he wanted to arrange it so. And thus it also came about that Mao-Tse-tung proclaimed the new united State, the People's Republic, in Peking.

Peking has become young again. From the comfortable, so bewitching leisureliness of a whole city — we know what poverty, what want, what despair, lay hidden behind these friendly façades — from this leisureliness has grown the tense march of a youth with its eyes on the future. While, too, the long-lasting iniquity — and, at times, terror — of a totalitarian domination should not be overlooked, one will quickly agree in this: youth not only marches in closed ranks but draws on an innate impulsion when, for example, they parade before their "President" in festive procession, who stands high aloft on the balustrade of the T'ien-an-men. This cannot immediately compare with the scene on the Red Square in Moscow. This one is less experienced, more naive and more colourful — one might almost say more human. Scarcely any of the Western observers who have had the opportunity to witness the festive procession on May 1 or October 1 (the National Foundation Day) have not been able to resist the force of the impression.

Peking today consists of four parts. These are: the almost square inner city, called the Tartar City because it was once reserved for the Manchurian Lords of China, in which stands the old Imperial Palace as the "innermost city"; then the south city, equally walled but with walls not quite so high, for the better differentiation of which it was called the Chinese City (once the district for amusement and variegated leisureliness); then the industrial city growing up east of the inner city (not only factories but also three- and four-storeyed blocks of workers' dwellings, shops, banks and swimming-baths have been conjured up there); and, finally, the western suburb, west of the inner city, which as recently as the time of the Japanese military domination has been called the "new" Peking. There stand the universities, the new hospitals, the administrative buildings, the zoo; from there you travel to the last Empress's "Summer Palace" that seems to be developing into a "cultural park of the masses"; and from this western part of the city you reach the Ming tombs, the burial-place of the Emperors of the Ming dynasty (1368—1644), who were fundamentally the originators of the Peking that we see today.

So the old Peking, in its double square walls, is embedded in a rapidly growing new Peking that has already exceeded the three million population figure. To a certain degree, this new Peking has become the nerve centre of the whole empire such as it never was before, not at the time of the Emperor Yung-lo, the founder, not under K'ang-hsi, the contemporary and counterpart of Peter the Great, and not under Ch'ien-lung, who refused trade relations with the English King, George III.

From the point of view of communications, Peking is in no way so favoured by the surrounding countryside as one might expect for the capital of the most populous country on earth. It consisted, indeed, at first of a small fort on the northern edge of the Chinese lowlands, the headquarters of the "Boundary Command North" of the T'ang dynasty (618—907). Only hesitantly, and entirely following great rulers' display of might, did the capital develop. The canal had to be extended here to ensure connection with the richer districts in central and southern China. Three main roads then branched off from Peking: to the west and south-west, the old road over the mountains in the province of Shansi and along the upper course of the Hwangho; to the north, over the Nankou pass, following the camel caravan route into the broad stretches of Mongolia; and to the northeast, the old military road over Shan-hai-kuan ("blockhouse between mountain and sea") to virgin Manchuria. Today, railways have long since been running to these parts of the empire. Towards the south, a railway-line runs via the two-million-peopled town of Tientsin and on to Nanking and Shanghai and on along the edge of the Shansi mountains to Wuhan and Canton, and from there to Hongkong. The construction of an extensive road network is still a task for the future. But many intersecting airlines see to it that Peking is once again developing to an international focal point such as it already was 650 years ago.

Like the old city, the broad roads which stretch out towards the cardinal points still show signs of their former size. One must certainly not imagine them as asphalted highways of the past. Only those leading in the vicinity of the Palace were paved with great squares of stone; the aspect of the others changed according to the weather. Dust clouds swirled under the strong winds of the year and the rains turned the streets into stretches of mud. This meant little to the grand people of the Court and the Imperial Administration, for they rode on horseback or were carried in palanquins. Over the holes in the roads the tradesmen drove their two-wheeled mule-waggons. From time to time, somewhere on the fringe of the city the camel caravans discharged the loads of wares they had brought, often from far distances, to take others off with them. There is little to be seen of that today. So far, traffic has not developed in density to the extent it has in other Asiatic metropolises, e. g., in Tokyo or Bangkok, but that is only a question of a few years until the domestic motor-car production can match the country's needs. In the meantime, one sees automobiles mostly of Russian or Czech origin, with also, here and there, new models from West European countries. Many of the old and new streets look almost empty: pedestrians go along them in groups; the three-wheeled taxi-droschkys, called "Pedicabs" by foreigners, are part of the street picture; while the good old bicycle is an indispensable means of transport. In the side-streets, the "Hutung", the picture might, indeed, correspond with the old times. On one-wheeled push-carts the retail-traders peddle their wares from corner to corner, singing their always-to-be-recognised verses, and now and again will open one of the house-doors that break up the window-less walls that are more than the height of a man. People come and go, here and there a bicycle, a squeaking manure-waggon. It seems to be just as it always was.

If we enter one of the premises, when we go through the outer door we find ourselves at first only in a new lane that is shut in on the far side by a low building. This is not yet the living quarters. We have to go through yet another doorway, coming out into another alleyway which provides a glimpse into a little courtyard. And only now do we see the main courtyard, laid out in the form of a square fringed with houses all melting one into the other — only a ground-floor with a built-out knee-high passage-way on which stand the columns that seemingly support the roof. The windows are wooden lattices with white paper pasted on them, the lattice-work being patterned into pretty, quadrangular, extravagant forms. A few flowers and shrubbery stand in the yard, everything very simply contrived. Towards the back, a still smaller subsidiary yard, in which are the kitchen and larders, forms part of the premises. The noise of the street penetrates only very subduedly here. In the midday sun some pigeons, to which little whistles are attached, flutter across the pale-blue sky. This gives a light whirring sound, irrevocably linked with Peking memories.

Let us turn back once more to the city. The picture of it imprints itself quickly. In the centre is always the Imperial Palace — the "Old Palace", as the Chinese call it. Towards the south rise the three mighty gateway-towers of the Ch'ung-wen-men (formerly called Ha-ta-men), the Ch'ien-men ("Foremost Gateway", picture 1) and the Hsüan-wu-men. The word "men" means "gate". To the east, north and west, two of the old gateway-towers each are to be seen, where in the meantime the city wall has been newly pierced in many places to make room for the growing traffic. The blue line of the western mountains, visible on fine days from the top of the Coal Hill (picture 11) or from the White Stupa in Pei-hai-Park (picture 14), is incomparable.

Both these belonged to the former Imperial City, which still, indeed, enclosed the actual, the "Forbidden City". As early as the period of the Chin dynasty — that is, still before the Mongols — the rulers had great basins of lakes constructed out of the swampy meadows and the excavated slime formed into a hill which was then planted with trees and decorated with gay little tea-pavilions. Around the lakes were arranged gardens, little temples, restrooms, gangways for boats — the whole set up as a place of recreation for the Imperial Court. The Ming rulers also had a hand in it. They restored what had fallen into decay, extended and built further. The Manchu rulers, too, left their traces, so that there is today an attractive chain of three medium-sized lakes, called the "northern, central and southern seas". The Stupa on the hill in the middle of the "northern sea" (that is, the Pei-hai) dates from the time of the last dynasty. It is the sign of the Tibetan Lama influence that was noticeable for a time, to which the great Lama temple in the northeast of the inner city can also bear witness.

The gateway towers of the inner city, the Coal Hill and the Pei-hai Stupa are — apart from the many tall blocks of flats that have shot up as the new Peking — the most noted sights for the foreign visitor. He should not, however, forego the view from the Coal Hill towards the north, for it looks out directly on to the broad and massive so-called Drum Tower standing there, the sole building testifying to the Mongol period, that characterises the picture of the north part of the city. And far towards the south, above the more lofty wall of the inner city, almost as far as the southern outer wall, it is the Temple of Heaven that catches the eye — that restrained, sweeping, three-stepped circular structure which, with its deep-blue glazed tiles and the golden gleaming roof "knob" is as well-known as the Eiffel Tower or Cologne Cathedral. (For this reason a photograph of it is not included in this volume.)

But to return to the centre, to the Palace! By way of the T'ien-an-men, the "Gate of Celestial Peace" (picture 3), we come to a broad square through the middle of which runs the road, surfaced with wide, square blocks. Diagonally across stands another and wider gateway-tower, with five passage-ways in the wall, the Tuan-men (picture 4), beyond which the road leads to the "Noontide Gate", the most massive gateway structure in the world. It is so named since, viewed from the Forbidden City, it lies exactly to the south, where the sun

13

is at noon. Here begins the "Forbidden City", the "Great Inner" as it was usually called in the old Imperial days, surrounded by a moat (picture 5). Passing through, we come again to a courtyard (picture 6) that this time is a broad as it is long with, in the foreground, five marble bridges rising above a waterway, the "Gold River". Further behind on a marble terrace there is another building which is again only a gate and entrance to the next court that really is now the centre of the whole — the "Hall of Great Harmony", where once gala audiences were received on special occasions. Two further halls follow behind, all three on the same marble terrace that towers above the rest of the palace grounds. And only when we have crossed a wide connecting court do we reach the private quarters of the Palace, where the Imperial Family once dwelt, where the Imperial concubines once had their quarters, with the eunuchs and the great concourse of servants and waiting-women.

Today all is open. The visitor goes from court to court, gateway to gateway, hall to hall, sighing a little, especially when the summer sun burns down, feeling that the palanquins must have been a pleasanter mode of progression, and letting himself be gripped by this creative force of a great mediaeval power. It is a subdued emotion: these blandly curving roofs breathe peace; everything is shaped into one harmonious picture — the yellow roof-tiles, the white marble terraces, the deep-red wooden columns, the broad sky, to whom the Emperor, the "Son of Heaven", too, was subject. This is China, as it has developed out of the centuries. The Government is well advised to try to preserve this unique monument. It makes use of the available space in order to display the opulence of Chinese culture before the descendants living today. One day there will be here a museum town of unbelievable beauty and variety.

Outside pulses life, the young life of the second half of the 20th century. Ten years it is now since Communist Party troops went speedily from victory to victory, to win over the whole country in, even for themselves, a surprisingly short time. Ten years since Peking could once again rightly bear its name as a capital. Ten short years, which scarcely assert themselves against a century of revolutionary outbreaks and slowly tormenting transformation. Compared with the centuries-old history they are as a tiny glint of light in the twilight. If one always bears that in mind one learns to be careful in judgment. New life pulses, above all in dozens of training-centres similar to our universities, in teacher training establishments, colleges and medical academies. Outside, before the western gates, lies the technical university — the former Tsing-hua academy. With an illimitable fervour students engage in machine-building, electro-technics, mining, architecture, the technique of oil extraction. Most of the text-books are Russian, and Russian is foreign language No. 1. In Russian even the secrets of nuclear techniques are elucidated. The lecture-rooms are full, the teaching-staff overtaxed. A deficiency in teachers, discernable since the very beginning of the new start, has still not yet been overcome. With persistent assiduity they copy, imitate, repeat, making an attempt here and there at improvement. It seems as if a whole people has got together on the bench at school.

About the schools and the blocks of dwellings youths and girls, not long in their teens, bustle about the sports-grounds. Team-games with a ball are much favoured, but light athletics, swimming and gymnastics have many adherents. Here and there a group squats together, earnest in conversation. Everything is new; only a first step; full of expectation for the future. Here and there they indulge in a cheerful pastime — singing, chaffing, shaking with scarcely irresistible laughter. At the back of it all there are also doubts, tormenting unrest, much uncertainty as to where the too-powerful State will order them when things have gone far enough. In the background there are also sharp disputes, which do not always end as satisfactorily as can seem from the outside. But what is that, ten years from the new start? Has not an unbelievable transformation already taken place? "From here to Hsinkiang sounds the same music", mused Mao, the President, "it never was so before." And the consciousness of living at the centre of a gigantic empire with still greater future prospects must give an inner support to the inborn submissiveness to the vicissitudes of life.

But we must be on our way. Along the magnificent street before the "Gate of Celestial Peace" one goes west to the entrance to the government quarter, to the buildings of the National People's Congress, of the People's Council, of the State Council. Somewhere about here the President, too, has his official quarters and the few men who hold in their hands the fate of 600 million people meet. Eastwards the same street leads to the Peking Hotel, one of the buildings towering high over the flat roofs and as well known to visitors to Old China as well as to the New. Today it has doubled in extent. Delegates from practically every country in the world make a rendezvous here. The sober suits of the European-influenced world mingle with the multi-coloured raiment of Asia and Africa. It is a habit to give receptions here, unique in noisy festiveness. Titbits from all the menus of China, drinks made from the juice of grapes and burnt rice stimulate the emotions; toasts follow one another

16

Die Ch'ien-men-Straße mit dem Außentor des Ch'ien-men
La rue Ch'ien-men et la porte extérieure du même nom
Ch'ien-men Street with the outer Gateway of the same name

Der Kaiserpalast — vom Kohlenhügel aus gesehen
Le Palais Impérial — vu de la Colline du Charbon
The Imperial Palace, as seen from the Coal Hill

Das T'ien-an-men, Haupteingangstor zum Kaiserpalast
T'ien-an-men, porte principale du Palais Impérial
The T'ien-an-men, the main entrance to the Imperial Palace

Das Tuan-men
Le Tuan-men
The Tuan-men

Wassergraben und Maueraufbauten des Wu-men
Fossé et murs de la Port Wu-men
Rampart-ditches and walls of the Wu-men Gate

Marmorbrücken über den „Goldfluß" in den inneren Palast
Ponts de marbre sur la Rivière de l'Or (intérieur du Palais)
Marble Bridges over the "Gold River" in the inner Palace

Eingangstor zur Porzellanausstellung
Porte d'entrée de l'exposition des porcelaines
Entrance to the Porcelain Exhibition

Kostbare chinesische Porzellanvase

Précieux vase de porcelaine chinoise

Valuable Chinese Porcelain Vase

Vergoldetes Fabeltier
Animal fabuleux doré
Gilded Mythical Animal

19492

Der kaiserliche Audienzthron
Le trône impérial des audiences
The Imperial Audience Throne

Pavillon auf dem „Kohlenhügel"
Pavillon sur la Colline du Charbon
Pavillon on the Coal Hill

Winterliche Kaiserstadt
Imperial City in winter
Dans la cité impériale en hiver

Dreitoriger Ehrenbogen im Pei-hai-Park
Arc de Triomphe à trois portes au Parc Pei-hai
Three-doored Triumphal Arch in Pei-hai Park

Die weiße Stupa im Pei-hai-Park

Le Stupa blanc du Parc Pei-hai

The White Stupa in Pei-hai Park

Vorbau der weißen Stupa
Construction avancée du Stupa blanc
Fore-part of the White Stupa

Die „Neundrachenwand" im Pei-hai-Park
Le mur des neufs dragons au Parc Pei-hai
The "Wall of the Nine Dragons" in Pei-hai Park

Fünftorige Ehrenpforte vor den Ming-Gräbern
Arc de triomphe à cinq portes précédant les tombeaux des Ming
Five-doored Triumphal Arch before the Ming Tombs

Steinerner Löwe an der Straße zu den Ming-Gräbern
Lion de pierre (Allée des Ming)
Stone Lion on the Road to the Ming Tombs

Opferaltar für Papiergeld im Grabbezirk
Autel votif pour monnaie de papier (Tombeaux des Ming)
Votive Altar for Paper Money in the Tomb Enclosure

Gedächtnispavillon im Grabbezirk
Pavillon du Souvenir (Tombeaux des Ming)
Memorial Pavilion in the Tomb Enclosure

Kassettendecke im Gedächtnispavillon
Plafond à caissons au Pavillon du Souvenir
Panelled Ceiling in the Memorial Pavillion

Innenraum eines buddhistischen Tempels
Intérieur d'un temple bouddhiste
Interior of a Buddhist Temple

Der „Sommerpalast" (I-ho-yüan)
La Palais d'Eté (I-ho-yüan)
The "Summer Palace" (I-ho-yüan)

Das Kaiserliche Theater
im „Sommerpalast"

Le Théâtre Impérial au
Palais d'Eté

The Imperial Theatre in
the "Summer Palace"

Eingangsbogen am See im „Sommerpalast"
Arc d'entrée (Lac du Palais d'Eté)
Entrance Arch in the "Summer Palace" Lake

Buddhastatue mit Schutzgottheit und Jüngern
Statue de Bouddha avec divinité protectrice et disciples
Statue of Buddha with Tutelary Deity and Disciples

Gedeckte Promenade im „Sommerpalast"

Promenade couverte (Palais d'Eté)

Covered Promenade in the "Summer Palace"

Pekinger Stadtmauer bei der alten Sternwarte

Les murs de la ville près de l'Ancien Observatoire

Peking Town Wall near the Old Observatory

Pekinger Himmelsglobus aus dem Jahr 1674
Sphère céleste pékinoise de 1674
Peking Celestial Globe, dating from 1674

Die „Chinesische Mauer" mit Befestigungstürmen
La Grande Muraille de Chine et ses tours de protection
The Great Wall of China with Defensive Towers

in rapid succession; and music, over everything, fuses all in one gala community drinking a health to the peace of the world represented in the capital of China.

Not far away, on both sides of a street that runs not east-west but north-south, are the most important shops of the old and the new capital. The Wang-fu-ching Street is for Peking what the Ginza is for Tokyo. Here are crowded far more people than in the rest of the city. Here, too, are to be seen foreigners who, mingling with the stream of passers-by, pass in front of the business-stalls, pausing here, going there to purchase something, until finally giving in to the attraction of the "Peking Bazaar". Through a lonely gate of modest appearance, on the grating of which is a more-than-life-size portrait of President Mao, under which you can read the four characters "Tung-an-shih-ch'ang" (Eastern Peace Market), you come to the paradise of the small trade. Here people move slowly along, young people, old men, women on the look-out for some object that has long become a necessity. Shoes, clothing, new and second-hand, pictures, pots and pans, postage stamps — everything the heart desires is displayed on the little, sometimes quite tiny, stalls. The twilight atmosphere of a covered market-place unites the very mixed crowd of buyers and sellers into one harmonious mass of people. Further along the street you come across books in many languages, but first and foremost in the colloquial tongue, now elevated to script. The language of Peking is today that of the whole of China. Only seldom do we remind ourselves that the change-over, by which the classical written language — to be mastered patiently and available only to the few arrivistes and literati — became the language of the people, has taken place only during the course of the present generation. This, too, is new. Beside the long and colourful shelves schoolchildren and students are deep in thought, pondering on providing themselves with this or that urgently-required textbook. Here is found Russian literature translated into Chinese, together with the French novelists of the 19th century, Heinrich Heine, Goethe, and, of course, the "classical exponents" of Marxism-Leninism. Here are found illustrated magazines telling of the new build-up in all parts of the country, of the mighty surge forward of the great Soviet Union. The "International Bookshop", as it modestly calls itself, is one of the most comprehensive book-publishing enterprises in the world. It publishes and handles everything that is newly printed, providing the written matter for the hectic learning-fever of a gigantic nation.

It is now a question of what is to be undertaken now. To turn north, to visit the Lama temple? For this a special permission is needed. Or shall we make a little excursion into another market-place of the city, in the south part of the town, the curiosity market of Liu-li-ch'ang? Perhaps, indeed, for the moment it is more exciting to accept an invitation to visit a modern hospital?

The building has a modern appearance, yet the slightly wavy roofs, glazed with green tiles, induce an unmistakable Peking atmosphere. Previously it was a hospital built and run by the Americans. In Chinese it was always called "Union Hospital" (Hsie-ho i-yüan), as though they had wanted already to suggest what they strive for today: a "more modern" fraternal association — that is, more or less Western medicine combined with the age-old methods of the Chinese medical art. Apart from the architect it is above alle the medical man, who has recourse to his own heritage. Yes: not seldom do they receive visits from foreigners who want to study their — Chinese — medicine.

A motor-droschky, in which one best crams oneself with several people because that is least time-wasting and cheapest, brings us into the south city.

Liu-li-ch'ang, the curiosity market! If you expect real articles of past ages you will be disappointed. These are good imitations of an old art, which comprehended how to work skilfully with metal and precious stones as with China's quite peculiar material — porcelain. We saw the real things this morning in the museum cases of the old Imperial Palace. Here is found what can be bought: an old copper kettle; a teapot, a relic of a Manchu family of the past; vases of all sizes; a basin for little goldfish; and old books, picture-scrolls and writing-scrolls, with the handwriting of a once less-known calligraphy. If you seek patiently, if perhaps you drink a cup of tea to bring the inclination to purchase into a proper perspective, you will find something that gives you pleasure. Later on it will preserve a remembrance for you, if you are receptive to certain moods, a smile from the depths of centuries. The gentle magic that let the Road to the East, to the Far East, seem so desirable to us, allows us still to experience it.

To allay our hunger, let us go into one of the little restaurants that here, in the south city, are not infrequent. Since Chinese cuisine is starting to spread to all places in Europe, we are already somewhat familiar with the handling of the two chopsticks that one takes in the right hand, a little clumsily at first but then with growing sureness, to dip into the bowl of meat, to pluck out the bean-seeds, to slide to the mouth the crisply over-baked pieces of sour-sweet fish. Today, hygiene is written large. The kitchens place value on being white-tiled and the chefs wear the international garments of their friendly guild — the broad white apron and the white chef's cap. But as ever they turn the noodles with that incomparable verve that hosts of tourists have already admired.

And now it is high time to return to the hotel in order to take part the next day in the trip to the Ming tombs. This takes us out through the northwest gate along a well-constructed road until we are greeted already from far off by a five-doored ceremonial gate. The mountains come nearer, bare and craggy and yet affably serene in their summery blue-green. Here the road is beset by animal figures, lions, camels, elephants, guarding the way to the graves. And, finally, the tombs themselves. One must know that this is the opposite to the "emotion" of the Palace. Here a great secular Power, that always felt itself in union with cosmic strength, created a cemetery that is, for its part, unique. Not like the Egyptian pyramids, high and lonely in the desert, but spaciously embedded in the landscape, the places effuse a peaceful calm. At times the tomb itself is only a simple mound of earth, high, certainly, but without much artificial embellishment. Before and beside stand the memorial halls and pavilions, in quiet gardens. Pines and maples are intent on maintaining peace. A whole dynasty, that reigned for more than 275 years, lies here at rest. Forgotten are the troubles, the catastrophes, the historical vicissitudes of a great Asiatic Power. Only their ultimate building design allows an impression of what powers were here released and, at the same time, joined together.

By comparison, the Summer Palace is "new fashioned". The building design of a great woman dominated here. One perceives that this is a later period. But, unconcerned, the youth of Peking frolics about in the grounds and especially on the lake. Boats load up for pleasure-trips. On fine summer days the shores resound with the hubbub of bathers. Not much farther, and one comes to the western mountains that have always beckoned from the distance. At their feet and in their ravines are enchanted temples, testimonies still to a rich Buddhist past. Somewhat more to the south flows the Yung-ting-ho with, over it, a famous bridge called by foreigners the "Marco Polo Bridge". On it was sparked off that fateful armed conflict between China and Japan in the train of which the second World War broke out.

The memories are still so fresh that the new Peking evokes. And that is perhaps what is decisive, in that this summarises all: as young as looks this Peking of today, its face towards the future, as ancient the foundations on which it stands. There are few places on earth in which past and future are so directly intertwined as here.

TO THE PICTURES

Ch'ien-men Street with the outer gateway of the same name

If one approaches from the south the main gateway in the wall of the former Tartar City, the "Foremost Gate" (Ch'ien-men), one is walking towards the outer gate built out towards the south, at one and the same time a fortification and an embellishment of the capital. Were it not to stand there, compact and with the graduated roof-edges looking so typical to us, the street could be anywhere else, at least in Japan where the same writing characters would be seen. The majestic breadth (one may with right use the word here) is characteristic of the main thoroughfares of Peking and it is at the same time the central axis of the whole city. To the north, behind the gateway-tower, the gates and palace halls of the former "Forbidden City" will open to us, while behind us the street runs away to the south, by the Temple of Heaven and off into the expanse of the North Chinese plain. The traffic still seems scanty but that has already changed and will soon be as dense as that in the other capitals of the world.

The Imperial Palace, as seen from the Coal Hill

When you have behind you the whole road from the Ch'ien-men and then gone through the Imperial Palace towards the

52

north, when you have climbed the moderately high so-called Coal Hill which in Chinese is called the "Look-out Hill" (Ching-shan) and then turned back, this is the imposing prospect that opens out before you. Like golden-brown billows the roofs of the Palace spread out between the green of the trees of life, gingkos and plane-trees. The view is exactly along the central axis in a southerly direction. The wall encloses the former "Forbidden City"; this is its northern limit. On the slopes of the "Coal Hill", that was once called the "Hill of Ten Thousand Years", you can see the tree on which the unlucky and last of the Ming Emperors hanged himself in 1644 when the rebels conquered capital and Palace.

"The Great Union of the Peoples of the World — Ten Thousand Years!" Here is where the masses pass by when they celebrate May 1 or October 1, the day of the foundation of the "People's Republic". Above, behind the marbled balustrade, the "Committee" and their closest collaborators, together with individual high-ranking foreign guests, customarily watch the procession marching down there before them. Below, right, you can see the wooden stands that usually accommodate the mass of foreign guests. Marble columns and marble bridges soaring above the gateway-structure are witnesses to a rich past.

The Tuan-men

The T'ien-an-men, the main entrance to the Imperial Palace

at the same time the national symbol of New China. "The Chinese People's Republic — Ten Thousand Years" reads the lettering on the left and that on the right

Once again it is a gateway that you have to go through if you want to reach the courtyards of the former Imperial Palace from the direction of the T'ien-an-men. It is similar to the larger outer gateway and only slightly lower, a little less projecting and more modest in pretension

53

and appearance. With what sensitivity the old master-builder has defined the nuances here! There are still five entrances, the centre one the largest. Through this only the Emperor himself was borne. The courtyard is already cut off from the outside world. It is quieter and more intimate than the massive fore-court that leads out to the public. Grass still growing between the stones gives the mighty structure something intimate.

Rampart-ditches and walls of the Wu-men gate

The next stage on the road to the inside of the former Imperial Palace is the Wu-men, the "Noontide Gate". Viewed from the front, it is the mightiest gateway-structure within the Palace confines. Both right and left of the main building, that is also built in the style of the other two gateways, stands a square gateway-tower. This view from the west side shows one of the corner-towers and the gable of the main hall. To the right stretches the western fore-wall of the gate with the one-storey corridor. Surrounded by a moat, on which occasionally there is a boat sailing, the structure slumbers in the peace of noontide, to which it owes its name. Here begins the innermost of the inner, the actual Imperial City.

Marble bridges over the "Gold River" in the Inner Palace

At last the actual Palace grounds disclose themselves. The Wu-men is gone through. The first great fore-court is reached. It is traversed by an artificial stream, flowing in marble, the so-called "Gold River". People nowadays are free to go for a walk over the centre of the five marble bridges where once only the Emperor's palanquins could be borne. Paved the whole length with marble squares, the road leads to the "Gate of High Harmony" (T'ai-ho-men) that hides the view of the main hall of the Palace, the "Hall of High Harmony" (T'ai-ho-tien). All who sought an audience of the "Son of Heaven" were conducted through here.

Entrance to the Porcelain Exhibition

Somewhere in the northeast of the Palace grounds, where formerly the women's quarters and the eunuchs' dwellings lay, there is now a Porcelain Exhibition. Once again a gatehouse gives entrance into the courtyard in which the buildings stand. All old Chinese houses are laid out in this manner, though simpler and more modest in their proportions. The style in which roofs, walls and marble stairs are carried out is always the same. But there is never the feeling of monotony. Rather, the great similarity of form induces the feeling of expanse and deliberate calm. Now and again the propensity to many-coloured decoration in the tiniest space has been able to succeed. Glowing colours, powerfully applied, need not disturb the quiet harmony.

Valuable Chinese Porcelain Vase

Not by accident do the English-speaking peoples call porcelain by its own name: "China". Already a white fragment among the finds made in connection with the excavations of the Shang capital (ca. 1200 B. C.) hints of early attempts in the production of porcelain. The collections of Chinese porcelain are renowned all over the world — the pure and genuine classical forms of the Sung (960—1279), the blue-white of the Ming (1368—1644) and the multi-colour of the K'anghsi (1662—1722) and Ch'ien-lung (1736—1796) periods. This massive vase could belong to one of the later periods.

Gilded mythical animal

Around the main hall of the Palace, on marble pedestals in bronze stand the animals of good augury — the slender crane, the long-lived turtle, with its back-armour like the vault of heaven, and the fabulous creature whose appearance signified the greatest luck in old legends. This two-horned scaly ant-eater with the hooves of an ox is called the "Ch'i-lin", and according to tradition it is really a unicorn. A variant of this could indeed be expressed here. The quality of the animal is human goodness because it is prepared to attack evil and yet cause harm to no one. It appeared, so the legend tells, when Confucius was born.

The Imperial Audience Throne

Today part of the many-branched museum, once the place from which great official audiences were given. The daily governmental business was performed elsewhere. Here appeared the Court in ceremonious pomp, the officials each according to rank, and the foreign "bringers of tribute" had to fall on their knees.

Pavilion on the "Coal Hill"

"Behind" the Palace, i. e., to the north, rises the "Look-out Hill", that Chinese popular speech, presumably through misunderstanding, called the "Coal Hill". On the top of it is found the biggest of the five pavilions that embellish it. From

here over a bowl of tea you can enjoy a panoramic view over the whole city. To the west on the finest days you can see the western mountains.

Imperial City in winter

In one of the many subsidiary courts of the extensive Imperial City another new exhibition has been opened. It is visited by school-children and families come to have a look at it. But often the most interesting seems to be something other than what one "must" see.

Three-doored triumphal arch in Pei-hai Park

Formerly the park was part of the Palace grounds. Today it is one of the best-loved popular parks. Such triumphal arches, called "P'ai-lou" ("structure with commemorative tablet"), are found at many spots. They were set up to honour a man who had rendered good service or to commemorate an important event.

They provide handsome decorations that give the place a friendly atmosphere.

The White Stupa in Pei-hai Park

It was called, not quite appropriately, the "Pei-hai-Pagode", since it is only a Stupa, symbol of a Buddhistic sacred relic such as are up particularly in Tibetan and Mongolian lamaism. From the tip of an island in the north sea (Pei-hai) you can get a magnificent view of all parts of the city from all angles. On the lake, once overgrown with lotus, today clerks and students enjoy themselves in their free time.

Fore-part of the White Stupa

The tiny temple that the previous picture already showed is this fore-part, the outer wall of which shows little figures of Buddha in ceramic. Inside is housed the lamaistic God of Death "Yamantaka", whose multi-armed figure, with its many terrifying faces imposed one on top of the other, provides an unusual contrast to the serene beauty of the rest of the park.

The "Wall of the Nine Dragons" in Pei-hai Park

The Wall of the Nine Dragons is also one of the many sights worth seeing. In green-glaced tiles are fashioned nine differently coloured dragons, the animals that symbolise Heaven and the power of the Central Lord. They are playing on the waves of the sea with the stars.

Five-doored triumphal arch before the Ming tombs

When you go northward from the west city you finally come to the neighbourhood of the burial-place taken up by the dead rulers of the Ming dynasty. Well before you reach it rises this triumphal arch, at the beginning of the road that leads directly to it. The lay-out has a modest appearance without the green decoration that must once have surrounded it. Nevertheless, the harmonious symmetry of the proportions is consummately expressed.

Stone Lion on the road to the Ming tombs

The road to the graves is bordered right and left by animals hewn out of stone, who are intended to guard the way to the spirits. All are fashioned in a certain manner and succeed in their grandiose simplicity in expressing an exclusive design of purpose. They are animals from foreign parts, mythical creatures and others from home circles, such as the figures of officials, that line the entrance to the graves. The mountains come closer; the graves are not far away.

Votive Altar for paper money in the tomb enclosure

Every tomb consists of a complete temple lay-out, with an entrance door, main and side-halls and the actual burial mound. Everywhere there are centres for devotion and sacrifice. Here you can burn paper money — a symbolical act, that is supposed to provide the dead on the other side with sufficient means to live their lives in proportion to their standing.

Memorial pavilion in the tomb enclosure

The buildings in this burial enclosure are carried out in the style well-known from the city. Today everything is clean and well-contrived, where formerly all was weatherbeaten and decayed. The successive dynasties, when they came newly to power, have thus looked after the holy precincts of former ruling houses. In this is manifested China's unbroken ruling tradition, thousands of years old.

Panelled ceiling in the Memorial Pavilion

To decorate with gleaming colour is no blasphemy. In honouring dead rulers, everything can have a festive character. If another character of the same tenor is taken for the uppermost, the inscription could mean "Gate of the Receipt of Mercy" (Ling-en-men). Obviously an entrance leads from here to another room.

Interior of a Buddhist temple

Everywhere in the mountains and ravines west and northwest of Peking Buddhist temples have been established in the course of the centuries, when the capital was here. Some of them have already half fallen into decay, while others have remained in better condition. in the decades of the civil war. Today, much is done for them also in order to bring them back to their old and new magnificence. While the times are over when they dominated the cultural picture of China (somewhere from the 4th to the 10th century A. D.), they have been maintained in many districts. The holy sutras are read before the mysteriously gleaming statues of Buddha and Bodhisatva and sometimes an old woman burns incense there.

The "Summer Palace" (I-ho-yüan)

West of the city lies the world-famous "Summer Palace". Its present form is due above all to the last Empress, who from 1875 to 1908 ruled China almost as an absolute monarch. An almost too conscious richness of form and embellishment betrays a taste which is not quite sure. Nevertheless, it lies in extremely attractive surroundings; not far distant are the pagodas near the "Spring of the Precious Stones". In summer young people enjoy bathing where formerly no mortal might glimpse without the permission of the Court.

*The Imperial Theatre in the
"Summer Palace"*

The rich heritage of the past is where it remains accessible to mankind everywhere. "Here she lived, the great old woman", a mother could tell her daughter, "when your grandfather was still a young man." Here she had theatrical performances arranged for her. Perhaps there was much deliberating here as to how one could defend oneself against the constantly advancing "foreign devils".

If you row in a boat on the lake you also come by this place. Landing, you can reach, through this three-doored entrance, the "Hall of the White Clouds", one of the many pompous structures on the artificial hill of the "Summer Palace". From this side the inscription on the tablet reads "Gleaming Heaven", the word for Heaven being represented by a roof-arch made of jade. Here is peace and recreation for those who can find time for a trip in the environments of Peking.

Statue of Buddha with tutelary deity and disciples

In one of the many temples that are also worth seeing in the neighbourhood of the "Summer Palace", you stand before one of the many-fashioned outward shapes of the so-called Mahayana Buddhism, that has become the appointed direction of this world religion in East Asia. "Mahayana" means "Great Vessel", by which

one signifies the great capacity of a religion that can lead all men to salvation.

Covered promenade in the "Summer Palace"

One of the most famous and most photographed views is this promenade, many hundreds of yards long, whose rich carvings and magnificence of colour are unforgettable in the far-drawn perspective. Groups of sightseers are continually being conducted along it. Tourist parties abroad never neglect to visit it. A successful photograph with the colourful background is a precious souvenir: "Me, too, in the Summer Palace outside Peking!"

Peking Town Wall near the Old Observatory

On a site on the Peking city wall, in the southeast corner of the north city, is the Old Observatory. It is one of the testimonies to the fruitful contact between the aspiring civilisation of Europe and the Old Chinese world of culture. European missionaries of the Jesuit Order introduced to China at the beginning of the 17th century the newly evolved methods of mathematics, astronomy and cartography. After surmounting many a difficulty they succeeded in being appointed astronomers to the Imperial Court. Their duty was the exact observation of the heavens and the prompt reporting of special celestial happenings. At a suitable spot on the city wall the Emperor had this observatory set up for them.

Peking celestial globe, dating from 1674

The Italian Matteo Ricci (1552—1610) laid the ground for modern science in China. Above all, his strong points were mathematics and cartography. His successor was the German Johann Adam Schall (1611—1666) from Cologne. He was mostly an astronomer. He withstood the change, in 1644 from the Ming to the Ch'ing period and became a devoted servant of the first Emperor from the

Manchu House. His successor was the Flemish Ferdinand Verbiest (1623—1688). The lay-out of the observatory is above all due to him. These instruments, in particular the mighty bronze celestial globe, were set up in accordance with his plans. Europeans occupied the post of Court Astronomer until the 19th century. Eastern art and Western knowledge have joined in fraternal association with the installation of these instruments.

The Great Wall of China
with defensive towers

For thousands of miles the "Great" or "Chinese" Wall stretches from the east near Shan-hai-kuan as far as the Turkestan desert. The Chinese call it the "Ten Thousand Mile-long Wall". The first beginnings date from the 4th century B. C. The mighty ruler Ch'in Shih-huang (221 —210 B. C.), the unifier of China, joined the pieces individually existing to form one whole. But it was first in the two-and-a-half centuries of the Ming dynasty that the wall became what we can marvel at today. It was in that period that the "Central Empire" was menaced by the inroads of Mongolian and Manchurian cavalcades. The wall formed only the backbone of a well-thought-out defence system. A monstrous expenditure was necessary to protect the Empire. Today there is no use for it — a monument to the history of mankind.